Where Would I Be
Without You?

For permission requests, please contact the publisher at:
Mango Publishing Group
2850 S Douglas Road, 2nd Floor
Coral Gables, FL 33134 USA
info@mango.bz

For special orders, quantity sales, course adoptions and corporate sales, please email the
publisher at sales@mango.bz. For trade and wholesale sales, please contact
Ingram Publisher Services at customer.service@ingramcontent.com or +1.800.509.4887.

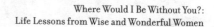

Where Would I Be Without You?:
Life Lessons from Wise and Wonderful Women

Library of Congress Cataloging-in-Publication Data
is available on request.
ISBN: (print) 978-1-57863-455-8
BISAC category code: BIO022000, BIOGRAPHY
& AUTOBIOGRAPHY / Women

Printed in the United States of America

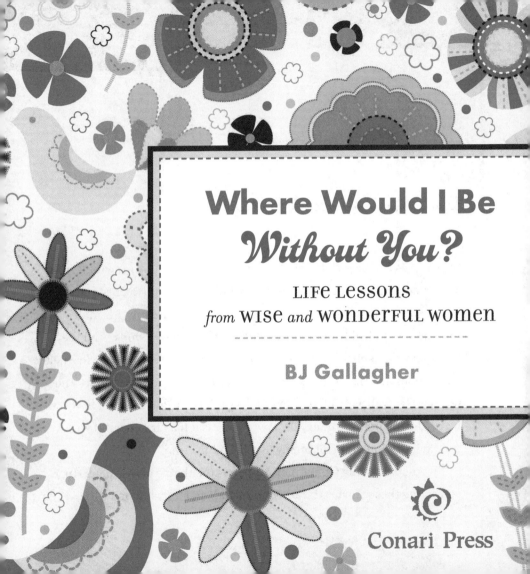

Where Would I Be Without You?

LIFE Lessons
from WISE and WONDERFUL WOMEN

BJ Gallagher

Conari Press

Introduction

When I was a little girl, I thought that when kids became grownups, they stopped changing—that adulthood was a state of stability. Once you grew up, I figured, that was it—you were you. But when I became an adult, I learned that I had been mistaken—the growing never stops. And the learning never stops . . . if I am open to it. Over the years, I have learned from books and newspapers, from movies and TV, from preachers and teachers, as well as from my own life experiences—but mostly I have learned from other women. Each woman has left a bit of herself with me—an indelible imprint on my psyche, on my soul.

Women learning from other women is the theme of this book. In compiling these stories, I wanted to include not only lessons from women in my own life, but from others' lives as well. I asked friends and family; I inquired among my professional colleagues; I sent out Internet queries; and I even pestered friends while we were vacationing together in Mexico. I asked lots of questions, like: **Where was it that you learned the important lessons of life?**

WHO are your teachers, your role models?

Where do you look to understand what it means to be a woman, how to live a fulfilled life, how to decide what's important, and what's the meaning of it all?

I hope the stories I have gathered in this book might help you live your life a bit happier, a tad healthier, and maybe with a smidgen more fun, too! True wisdom is the ability to learn from other people's experiences—without having to go out and reinvent the wheel. This book is my gift to you—may it bring you a little bit of wisdom and lots of inspiration.

With love and laughter,
BJ Gallagher

Attitude
Is Everything

NOBODY

can be exactly like me.

Sometimes even I have trouble doing it.

—Tallulah Bankhead, actress

Other women have taught me much about the critical role that attitude plays—in good times and in bad. Most importantly, they taught me that I can choose my own attitude! It's not something immutable in my DNA over which I have no control. My attitude is not cast in concrete— in any given moment, I can choose to change it.

Attitude is everything.

One of my mother's favorite sayings was

"MIND OVER MATTER."

She invoked this mantra whenever I was whining or complaining (as kids often do). "Mind over matter" was an all-purpose panacea for assorted and sundry problems. Feeling lonely? Instead of focusing on your aloneness as a problem, view it as an opportunity to do something that requires solitude, like writing or cleaning your closet. Make a gratitude list and see all the wonderful things you have going for you!

**What do you hang
on the walls of your mind?**

−Eve Arnold, photographer

LIFE IS raw material.

WE ARE ARTISANS.

We can sculpt our existence into something beautiful,
or debase it into ugliness. It's in our hands.

—Cathy Better, poet and writer

I WENT TO VISIT MY AUNTIE EL IN SEDONA A COUPLE OF YEARS AGO, AND OVER LUNCH ONE AFTERNOON, I COMMENTED ON HER BEAUTIFUL COLLECTION OF HATS. She smiled knowingly and leaned in to whisper something so that her husband wouldn't overhear: "I wear these stunning hats so people will look at my face and not my big tush!" she confided.

And she was right—that's exactly what people did.

NOTHING CONVEYS THE RIGHT ATTITUDE LIKE A GREAT HAT!

IF YOU OBEY ALL THE RULES

you miss all the fun.

—Katharine Hepburn, actress

What separates an ordinary woman
from an extraordinary one?
The belief that she is ordinary.

—Jody Williams, Nobel Peace Prize winner

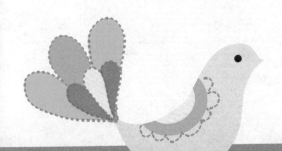

YOU, too, have the power to recreate yourself over and over again, as many times as you want. You can try on new identities much like you might try on a new coat, or experiment with a new hairstyle. The freedom you have as a new woman living in the western hemisphere at this point in history means you can be a tomboy, a scholar, a vamp, a pastor, a cynic, a party girl, a homebody, a hermit, or whatever else strikes your fancy. Your only limit is your creativity, imagination, and energy.

There is no cosmetic for beauty like

happiness.

—Marguerite Gardiner Blessington,
Irish writer

You don't have to decide what you're going to be, ever.
You can be something different every day if you want.

—*Laurie Anderson's mom*

we were once

WILD

Here.

Don't let them tame you.

—Isadora Duncan,
mother of Modern Dance

Where would I be if it weren't for my women friends?
We laugh together, cry together, compare notes on
our children, and complain about our jobs. I depend
on them for so much—company, comfort, guidance,
advice, and sometimes a good swift kick when I need it!

Our common bond of feminine experience is stronger
than any differences. There is something so essential in
women sharing with other women. It seems the most
natural thing in the world. Give me the support of a few
good women friends, and I can do almost anything!

My friend Suzanne once said to me,
"The greatest gift you can give someone is the gift of the interested listener."
Suzanne was right. Think about it. What is it we all want more than anything? We want to be heard, to be acknowledged, to have someone validate our existence, our thoughts, and our feelings. Like a bank account, friendships grow in direct proportion to interest paid.

Everything I Need to Know about Friendship I Learned from My Girl Friends

A True Friend, From **A** to **Z** . . .

ACCEPTS you, warts and all.

BELIEVES in your potential.

COMFORTS you when you're sad.

DELIGHTS in your successes.

EMPATHIZES with your struggles.

FORGIVES you when you hurt her feelings, just as you do her.

GIVES you time and attention.

HUGS you . . . often.

INSPIRES you to do your best.

JUST LOVES YOU.

KEEPS your secrets.

LISTENS with her heart.

MAKES you want to be a better person.

NEVER JUDGES YOU.

OCCASIONALLY DISAPPOINTS you 'cause she's human, too . . .

POINTS OUT your good qualities when you forget.

QUESTIONS you when you're about to do something really dumb.

RESPECTS your boundaries.

SHARES her hopes and fears with you.

TELLS you the truth.

UNDERSTANDS you, even when you don't understand yourself.

VALUES your ideas and opinions.

WILL DO anything she can to help you.

XTENDS a helping hand whenever you need it.

YEARNS to hear from you when you're away.

ZINGS with joy 'cause you're her friend.

"We need to allow other people the dignity of their own choices," my friend Karen told me. The dignity of personal choice—what a wonderful concept!—the essence of free will and self-determination. I certainly want it myself, and I must allow others to have it, too.

If we would build on a sure foundation
in friendship, we must love friends
for their sake rather than for our own.

–Charlotte Brontë, author

Women of our generation figured out we could try to have it all. We were smart, we went to school, we had careers, and we had families. We learned to be assertive and not aggressive. We learned to volunteer and make a difference. We learned when to say "No" to things that didn't matter to us personally and professionally.

What we didn't learn was how to say "YES." "Yes," I need help. "Yes," you can bring dinner over, sit with the kids, do my laundry, or just listen because, frankly, I can't do it all by myself. "Yes," I need others. Maybe what we need to do is say "No" to Superwoman more often, and say "Yes" to our friends instead.

Family:
Fun or Funky?

98%

of families
are dysfunctional.

THE OTHER TWO PERCENT ARE LYING.

—Amy Berger, humorist and author

STRUCTURE
Is
Love:

Kids learn much better by experiencing things than by someone telling them things. My mom knew that loving your kids doesn't mean letting them do whatever they want—it means giving them boundaries and guidelines within which to live and grow.

Sometimes there is a huge gap between the intent of a comment and its impact. It's easy to forget how sensitive my family members are—to unthinkingly hurt the ones I love the most.

I must speak more often from my heart, and less from my head.

If it's not one thing,
IT'S YOUR MOTHER.

—Gilda Radner, comedian

How women and men handle their money speaks volumes about their families: whether or not they feel loved, how they provide for their children, and ways in which they act out their relationships with other family members. Money is intertwined with issues of power, control, sex, self-esteem, love, and loyalty. Carolyn Wesson's book *Women Who Shop Too Much* showed me that hiding purchases is just one small example of how interpersonal issues show up in the family checkbook. It's important for families to take the mystery out of money.

Virginia Quirk told me,

Advice to children can be risky, and as ours matured,
we had a creed we adhered to:

**Never give adult children advice
unless they are asking for money.**

**If adult children *ask* for advice,
that's another story.**

It worked for us.
But in their developmental years, advice was needed—
after all, that's what parenting is all about.

Our children sometimes choose paths that we don't understand or approve of, but we must accept their right to choose for themselves.

Making Peace
with the Past

Childhood

is the first inescapable political situation
each of us has to negotiate. You are powerless.
You are on the wrong side in every respect.

BESIDES THAT, THERE'S THE SIZE THING.

—June Jordan, poet, novelist, and critic

The past is a weird thing. Somehow, it keeps showing up in the present. Even worse, sometimes it seems to predict the future! Old issues that we thought were finished show up disguised with new faces. Old wounds are reopened by new people . . . or sometimes by the same people who gave us the original wounds. Our fathers show up in our relationships with men. We're haunted by the fear that we might be turning into our mothers. Old parental issues get reenacted with authority figures like bosses. What's the deal here? More importantly, is there anything we can do about it?

A wise friend once told me

**UNTIL YOU GET COMPLETE WITH YOUR PARENTS,
YOU CAN'T GET COMPLETE WITH ANYONE.**

Her advice was this:

If you have unresolved issues with your parents, drop everything else you're doing and take care of that. If you don't then old garbage from the past will continue to clutter up your life and your relationships forever.

We all live in **SUSPENSE**
from day to day;
in other words, you are
the **HERO** of your own story.

—Mary McCarthy,
author of *On the Contrary*

It's time
to let parents
off the hook.

My mom told me,
**Blame your parents
for the way you are;
blame yourself
if you stay that way.**

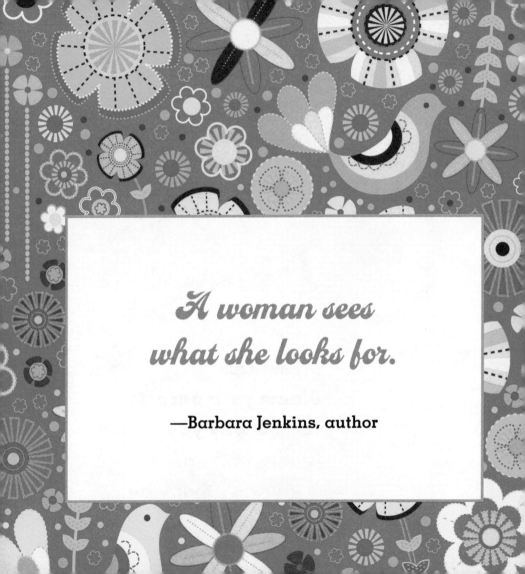

*A woman sees
what she looks for.*

—Barbara Jenkins, author

My friend Anita Goldstein said,

Every time you hear yourself making some blanket statement like, "I'm very insecure . . . I need a lot of attention and reassurance," I'd suggest that you add these three words, "up until now." Every time you do that, you're making a break with the past. You're giving yourself permission to change.

IT'S never too late
to become
what you might have been.

—George Eliot
*(Mary Ann Evans, who
wrote under a male pen name)*

My Body / My Self

Women's bodies are both beautiful and practical.
Our *soft curves and alluring femininity*
have for centuries inspired the world's greatest artists.
On the other hand, our innate physical durability enables
us to give birth to babies and feed them, work hard,
juggle multiple roles, and go the distance, outliving men.
Our bodies are nothing short of miraculous—the epitome
of **FORM FOLLOWS FUNCTION.**

Some of us are **not so thrilled** with Mother Nature's handiwork, though. In fact, I don't know a single woman who actually likes her body. Women worry and fret about being too fat, too tall, too short, too something! We worry about our health, aging, and the loss of physical beauty as well as the prospect of being old ladies in a society that worships youth. *Having a woman's body is definitely a mixed blessing.*

You can take no credit for beauty at sixteen. But if you are beautiful at sixty, it will be your soul's own doing.

—Marie Carmichael Stopes, Scottish writer

When I was a little girl, occasionally I got sick.
No matter what minor illness I had,
my mother would always say the same thing:

Wash your face — you'll feel better.

When you look better,

you'll feel better, too.

Women Educate Other Women about Our Bodies

We have been sharing information with one another for thousands of years—mothers and grandmothers taught younger generations about menstruation, sex, pregnancy, and other important female issues. Women friends have always shared with one another what they learned from their own experiences and illnesses.

We have the opportunity to share health information with the dozens of women we know and love. Armed with the latest facts from the Internet, doctors, books, journals . . . and Oprah . . . we can take charge of our own health and teach other women as well.

THE FIVE STAGES
of a WOMAN'S LIFE:

1. *To grow up*
2. *To fill out*
3. *To slim down*
4. *To hold it in*
5. *To hell with it*

Men and Marriage

Having a healthy relationship with a man means
loving him for who he is now,
and not loving him in spite of who he is today,
or in hopes of who he will be tomorrow.

—Barbara DeAngelis,
author and relationship expert

The woman's vision is deep reaching—
the man's far reaching.
With the man, the world is his heart;
with the woman, the heart is her world.

—Betty Grable, **actress**

TOP TEN THINGS I'VE LEARNED ABOUT MEN

1. Men are simpler than women are. What you see is pretty much what you get.

2. Men are single-focused. Don't expect them to multi-task.

3. Men need to be right. They like to win.

4. Men are either attracted to you or they're not. Don't go to great lengths to try to win a man who isn't attracted to you. Watch for the ones who are.

5. Men like the chase.

6. Most men have a much higher sex drive than women. It's biological—their bodies and minds are hardwired for frequent sex. It doesn't make them bad or dirty—it just makes them men.

7. Men want sex and trade intimacy to get it. Women want intimacy and trade sex to get it.

8. Many of men's emotions get expressed as anger. They've been socialized not to express other emotions. Fear comes out as anger; frustration comes out as anger; sadness comes out as anger; even jealousy comes out as anger.

9. Men need women. Most of them don't do well without us. They get sick more often, they make less money, and they die sooner without a woman in their lives. Most men know this.

10. Men love and want women, but they often don't understand us. They love us because we're so different from them—complex, paradoxical, emotional, expressive, beautiful. But the differences also confuse them. They sometimes don't know how to make us happy.

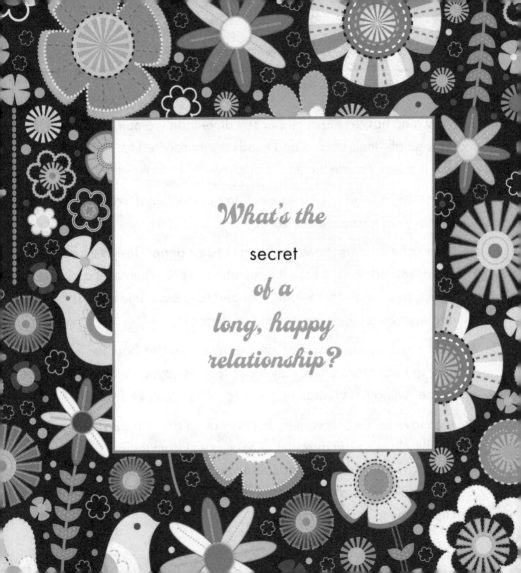

What's the

secret

of a

long, happy

relationship?

You have to strike the right balance between
time together and time apart.

Love is a great degree of tolerance.

The key to a long marriage is a short memory.

The ability to compromise and forgive
is essential to a successful marriage.

Hold each other close, with your arms open wide.

For a happy, successful marriage,
my friend Carole says,

**"The woman should love her man a little,
and understand him a lot;
and the man should love his woman a lot,
and understand her not at all!"**

I asked my friend Gwen about her long marriage.

"You shouldn't depend on one man to satisfy all your needs,"
she said. "I think every woman should have three men in her life:

a gay guy to enjoy the arts with,

a stud muffin for the bedroom,

and an athlete to bring you adventure and activity."

"What about a husband?" I asked.

"Oh, well, any one of those three could be your husband—
you decide," Gwen replied.

Men

just want to

make us

HAPPY.

My friend Alison Armstrong said,

Our men really do want to make us happy. But if they can't make us happy, they'll settle for not making us upset. . . . Too many women want their men to be mind readers. "If he loves me, he should know what I want!" we complain. Wrong! Men aren't mind readers. You can save yourself and your man a lot of headaches by simply telling him what will make you happy.

Thanks to Alison, I've learned not to make men guess. Heaven knows, men find women mysterious enough as it is—I try not to make the guys more miserable by asking them to read my mind. . . . Only other women can read my mind!

DO let him read the papers. But not while you accusingly tiptoe around the room, or perch much like a silent bird of prey on the edge of your most uncomfortable chair. (He will read them anyway, and he should read them, so let him choose his own good time.) **DON'T** make a big exit. Just go. But kiss him quickly, before you go, otherwise he might think you are angry; he is used to suspecting he is doing something wrong.

—Marlene Dietrich, actress

Let your husband wear the pants
in the family, but be sure to lay his
clothes out for him in the morning.

—Betty Barr, Phyllis Barr's mom

Women at Work

The problem with the rat race is that,

EVEN IF YOU WIN,

you're still a rat.

—Lily Tomlin, comedian, actress, author

WHAT IS WOMEN'S WORK? Some women see their work as building nests and raising the next generation. Some say their work is to make a difference and to build a better world. Some focus on putting food on the table and keeping the wolf from the door. Many of us say, "All of the above!"

We can learn much about work from other women, and much about ourselves—lessons of creativity and courage, in dealing with adversity, in conflict and collaboration, and in leadership. So much to learn, so little time! **WOMEN'S WORK HAS ALWAYS BEEN—AND PROBABLY ALWAYS WILL BE—24/7.**

The goal must not be to find a job,
BUT TO BECOME A MAGNIFICENT WOMAN.

—Marianne Williamson,
spiritual teacher, author

"If I could ask you only one question, what question should I ask to find out the most important things about you?" I asked the group I was teaching one day. "What question would lead me to the real essence of who you are?"

"Ask me about my art," one woman replied. "I am an artist, and my work is central to who I am. I don't exist without my art."

I was struck by her simple but powerful comment. It prompted me to think about the role of work in my own life. . . . Over the years I've changed, and today I live to work. I have a mission, a purpose, something larger than myself, and it isn't wrapped around another person. . . . How do you decide what's more important and what's less important?

For many women today, family comes first and everything else takes a back seat. For others, it is career first, with achievement and financial success at the top of their list. Remember: There is no right or wrong answer on this question—only choices.

What is the role of work in your life? Do you work to live? Are you like my student, and live to work? What's the most important question I should ask you—to find out who you really are?

Some women have told me that they dislike working for women bosses—they perceive women with authority as demanding, picky, controlling, competitive, and even mean. Other women say that they prefer working for women bosses—they are good listeners, they're smart, they share information, they're supportive, and they're good team players. Who's right? I think Golda Meir, the former Prime Minister of Israel summed it up nicely:

"Whether women are better than men I cannot say . . . but I can say they are certainly no worse."

Getting Good
at Getting Along

Standing
in the middle
of the road is
very dangerous;
you
get
knocked
down
by
the
traffic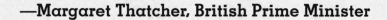
from
both sides.

—Margaret Thatcher, British Prime Minister

Don't compromise yourself.
YOU'RE ALL YOU'VE GOT.

—Janis Joplin, singer, songwriter

Speak up for yourself,

OR YOU'LL END UP A RUG.

—*Mae West, actress*

I bear **NO GRUDGES.**
I have a mind that retains
NOTHING.

–Bette Midler, actress, singer

LOVE YOUR ENEMY
—*it will drive him nuts.*

—Eleanor Doan, educator

My friend and fellow author Janelle Barlow taught me that a complaint is really a gift. Just like we thank someone who gives us a birthday gift, we should thank someone who brings us a complaint. They have given us something valuable, something useful, and something that can help make our business stronger and more profitable—we should treat their complaint as the gift that it really is. Complaints are simply a normal part of what it means to live in relationships with other people. . . . If we can hear what's behind the complaint—the desire to fix something that's hurting the other person—then we can see how their complaint really is a gift!

I have a simple philosophy:

Fill what's empty.

Empty what's full.

Scratch where it itches.

—Alice Roosevelt Longworth,
President Theodore Roosevelt's daughter

The world is all about relationships. Not just relationships between bosses and employees, but relationships between co-workers, relationships between friends, relationships with family members, and with neighbors. To paraphrase a well-known campaign slogan: "It's relationships, stupid."

LIFE IS ABOUT RELATIONSHIPS.

Thorns
among Roses

"All that is necessary to break the spell of inertia and frustration is this:

ACT AS IF IT WERE IMPOSSIBLE TO FAIL.

That is the talisman, the formula, the command of right-about-face which turns us from failure towards success."

—DOROTHEA BRANDE, AUTHOR

Someone wise once said,

CIRCUMSTANCES DON'T MAKE A PERSON'S CHARACTER, THEY REVEAL IT.

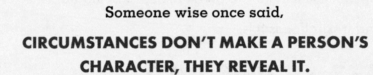

Maya Angelou wrote,

You may encounter many defeats,
but you must not be defeated.
In fact, the encountering may be
the very experience which creates the
vitality and the power to endure.

Humans are

social creatures,

and we do best when we

STICK TOGETHER.

The myth of the

RUGGED INDIVIDUAL

is just that—

a myth.

We could never learn to be brave and patient **if there were only joy in the world.**

—*Helen Keller, first deaf/blind person to graduate from college*

One of my friend Diana Barnwell's favorite sayings
from her mother is,

*There are no answers. . . .
Pursue them lovingly.*

In certain life situations, there is no good solution, no clear answer. There are only trade-offs, stand-offs, or stalemates. In such situations, the best one can do is to proceed with great caution, sensitivity, and loving kindness. There often is no "happy ending," and we must live with tension, anxiety, and lack of resolution. **LOVE IS THE ONLY GUIDING PRINCIPLE.**

Heart and Soul
of the Matter

Perhaps they are not stars in the sky, but rather openings where our loved ones shine down to let us know they are happy.

—Eskimo legend

My friend Barbara is among the growing number of women who have given up looking for love in all the wrong places. She explains:

All along what I really wanted was a friend, a hug, a smile, someone to talk to, someone who really understood me, someone to love me. I didn't know how to get those things, so I reached for things I did know how to get—food, alcohol, prescription pills, and new clothes. They were legal and easy to get, and they seemed to work. The problem is they didn't work long enough. I'd have to get another 'fix'. . . .

Once I found my way to twelve-step programs I found a solution. I found the hugs, smiles, listening ears, compassionate hearts, and the unconditional love that I had wanted all along.

Barbara and other women like her are teaching me how to look for love in all the right places.

I'm fulfilled in what I do. . . . I never thought that a lot of money or fine clothes—the finer things in life—would make you happy. My concept of happiness is to be filled in a spiritual sense.

—Coretta Scott King, civil rights activist

I learned from my friends that while our own personal definition of God is important to each of us as individuals, it is not what's important to us as friends. Our theology is not what brings us together—it's not the teachings of any particular priest, rabbi, minister, or guru that makes us spiritual sisters. Sharing our experiences with one another is what's really important to us as we continue to walk our spiritual paths. I suspect that all paths ultimately lead to the same place. **Many roads—one destination.**

THE TRUTH

is that there is only one terminal dignity—

LOVE.

And the story of a love is not important—

what is important is that one is capable of love.

It is perhaps the only glimpse
we are permitted of eternity.

—HELEN HAYES, ACTRESS

About the Author

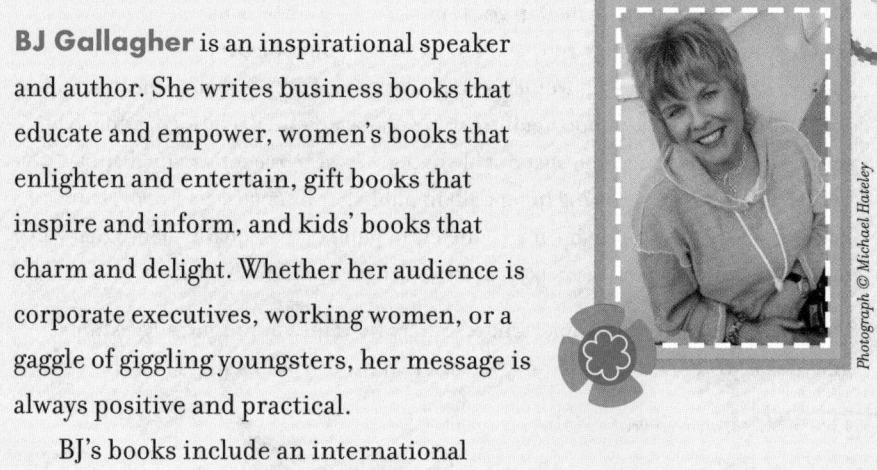

Photograph © Michael Hateley

BJ Gallagher is an inspirational speaker and author. She writes business books that educate and empower, women's books that enlighten and entertain, gift books that inspire and inform, and kids' books that charm and delight. Whether her audience is corporate executives, working women, or a gaggle of giggling youngsters, her message is always positive and practical.

BJ's books include an international bestseller, *A Peacock in the Land of Penguins*. Her newest women's book is *Why Don't I Do the Things I Know Are Good for Me?* She's also the author of *Friends Are Everything* and *Women's Work Is Never Done*, both published by Conari Press. She lives in sunny Southern California, the perfect place for a sunny personality who says "YES!" to love, laughter, and life. Visit her online at *www.womenneed2know.com*.

To Our Readers

Mango Publishing, established in 2014, publishes an eclectic list of books by diverse authors—both new and established voices—on topics ranging from business, personal growth, women's empowerment, LGBTQ studies, health, and spirituality to history, popular culture, time management, decluttering, lifestyle, mental wellness, aging, and sustainable living. We were recently named 2019 and 2020's #1 fastest growing independent publisher by *Publishers Weekly*. Our success is driven by our main goal, which is to publish high quality books that will entertain readers as well as make a positive difference in their lives.

Our readers are our most important resource; we value your input, suggestions, and ideas. We'd love to hear from you—after all, we are publishing books for you!

Please stay in touch with us and follow us at:

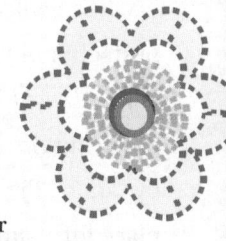

Facebook: Mango Publishing
Twitter: @MangoPublishing
Instagram: @MangoPublishing
LinkedIn: Mango Publishing
Pinterest: Mango Publishing
Newsletter: mangopublishinggroup.com/newsletter

Join us on Mango's journey to reinvent publishing, one book at a time.